Like A Butterfly!

Like A Butterfly!

Joan Wilson

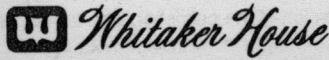

Unless otherwise indicated, all Scripture quotations are taken from the *New American Standard Bible*, © The Lockman Foundation, 1960, 1962, 1968, 1971, 1973, 1975, 1977, and used by permission.

Scripture quotations marked (NKJ) are from the *New King James Version*, © 1979, 1982 by Thomas Nelson, Inc. Used by permission.

Scripture quotations marked (AMP) are from the *Amplified New Testament*, © 1954, 1958, 1987, by the Lockman foundation, and are used by permission.

LIKE A BUTTERFLY

ISBN: 0-88368-295-8
Printed in the United States of America
Copyright© 1993 by Whitaker House

Whitaker House
580 Pittsburgh Street
Springdale, PA 15144

All rights reserved. No portion of this book may be used without permission of the publisher, with the exception of brief excerpts in magazine articles, reviews, etc.

Contents

Prologue 7
1. Why Don't You Like Yourself? 13
2. Why Do You Hurry So? 19
3. Let's Talk about Burdens 25
4. Let's Talk about Words 39
5. Almost Normal 49
6. The Baby Wakes 59
7. You Heard the Wrong Voice 63
8. Why Do You Harbor Hatred? 77
9. Wait on Me 87
10. The Window of Faith 95
11. The Meaning of Grace 105
12. Learning Me 115
13. Speak the Truth 121
14. Look Back with Me 129
15. The Listening Ear 137

Prologue

I was depressed....

Outwardly, I wore a smile—especially at church on Sunday—but inside, I was a mess. Then I met a dear Christian lady who saw right through my phony front, diagnosed the hurt, got down on her knees in my living room and started to pray.

Healing came, as all true healings do, in a flash of understanding—in seeing life not from my tiny peephole, but from God's grand view. I saw that all my hurts, whether caused by others or my sin, are used by God to fashion and form a new person, a new me!

The truth was liberating, and I jumped up from the couch. "Mary, I'm going to write a book some day, and I'm going to call it, *Lord, I've Felt Like a Worm for So Long, It's Hard to Think Like a Butterfly!*"

8 *Like a Butterfly*

We both laughed, reveling in the joy of the moment. Then she sobered and said, "I do think it would be a good idea for you to keep a daily journal. Write your thoughts, any Bible verses you find, your prayers—just whatever comes to mind. It will help you see what God is doing in your life, and it also will help you see your real self. You don't have the slightest idea who you really are."

Two weeks later, I sat in bed one night, reviewing my journal. The days when I managed to get my work done, be kind to everyone, pray, and read the Bible, were "good" days. If I yelled at the kids and didn't get much done, then it was a "bad" day.

While I was mulling over this self-imposed grading system, a thought came suddenly, penetrating my thoughts. It came as a question:

Why don't you like yourself?

The question intrigued me. Until that moment, I didn't know I didn't like myself. But it was true.

Since I had become accustomed to writing my thoughts, I jotted the question in my journal and then wrote a reply. Another question came, another reply, and not until I finished the conversation did I realize I had been talking with the Lord!

Astonishing! Had it really happened? Was it really the Lord Jesus talking or was I making it all up? Perhaps it was just one of those marvelous one-time miracles He gives when we need a special boost.

You can bet I was ready the next night, pen in hand, just in case it happened again. It did. Again, and as often as I would listen, He was ready to speak. Never audibly, of course, but always inside my thoughts, imparting truth I could never have imagined.

That was sixteen years ago. I wish I could say I have always been faithful since then to listen, but sometimes I lose faith to believe it is really Him. Sometimes I get very busy to avoid Him and the change that comes from hearing Him, because I have listened often enough to know the experience can be radically transforming.

10 *Like a Butterfly*

Listening is not just a safe, easy way to gain insights into Scripture. Listening causes confrontation with the only true revolutionary, the Person of Jesus Christ.

Listening is the *"good part"* (Luke 10:42) that Jesus commended Mary for choosing. In contrast, her busy sister, Martha, was corrected for worrying about all the work she had to do.

While Martha fretted and fussed, Mary sat quietly at the Lord's feet. I don't think she was sitting there taking notes, working on her theological degree. She just enjoyed being with Jesus. (See Luke 10:38-42.) Though she heard what He said, she was learning the Man. By being in His presence she was transformed—without doing anything at all!

I was asked, "What is your purpose in publishing your book?" My answer is that I want to inspire disciples of the Lord Jesus Christ. Though pastors and teachers are God's wonderful gift to us, if we depend only on them for our Christian teaching, then we are disciples of men and not the Man, Jesus. A true disciple is one who is taught personally by the Lord Himself.

I encourage every Christian, whether old or young, rich or poor, smart or simple, to dare to believe Jesus Christ can and will talk to them personally. After all, He promised, *"Behold, I stand at the door and knock. If anyone hears My voice and opens the door, I will come in to him and dine with him and he with Me"* (Revelation 3:20.)

This verse draws a picture. I see two people, at ease and enjoying the other's company. The next thought is so overwhelming I can hardly bear it. I see both seated on an equal level! I don't see one of them standing to serve or kneeling before the other, but instead two friends, beloved companions!

This is the heart of the Gospel. The good news is that Jesus Christ is not far off in heaven somewhere, way above us, lording it over us.

He is here now. Through His Spirit, He has taken a lowly place again and is sitting at the kitchen table of our hearts. He has come and made His home in us!

Joan Wilson

1

Why Don't You Like Yourself?

Why don't you like yourself?

I don't like people who like themselves, Lord. I work hard to keep myself from doing that.

Now that I think about it, the Bible says I should love my neighbor as myself. I guess I'm supposed to love myself so I can love others, but I don't like the thought. It just seems wrong and sinful. What should I do?

Do nothing. Let Me explain. You need to be released from your way of thinking and receive understanding from Me.

14 *Like a Butterfly*

Do you know of My love for our Father?

>Yes, Lord.

Do you consider that kind of love sinful?

>Of course not, Lord.

You are to love yourself in the same way.

>I don't understand.

I have time to explain. Do you have time to listen?

>Lord, I sense You are smiling, but I think You are reminding me of the reluctance I had to spend time alone with You. Are You saying I should take time to listen if You are willing to take time to talk with me?

Something like that.

>Okay, Lord, I'm listening. How do I love myself as You love our Father?

Why Don't You Like Yourself? 15

You often want a list of rules, but I'm speaking of a way.

What way, Lord?

The way I love our Father is as a part of Myself. This is the way He loves Me. He does not see Me as separate from Himself, and I do not see Myself as separate from Him. We are part of each other. When you can see more clearly, you will see that you, too, are part of Me.

This is not a theological theory, but fact. This is truth. This is reality, not something to be hoped for, worked for, or achieved by learning. It is fact. You are part of Me.

If you will make your chief aim to enjoy Me, that will include enjoyment of yourself as well.

Lord, I had a glimpse just then of liking and enjoying myself, and for the first time I understand why the Amplified Bible translates *"blessed"* in the Beatitudes as *"happy, to be envied, and spiritually prosperous [that is, with life-joy and satisfaction in God's favor and salvation, regardless of your outward conditions]"* (Matthew 5:11 AMP).

Won't my satisfaction bother some people? Won't they hate me for it?

You can count on it. If some hated Me, some will hate you. Living in the realm of reality provokes real responses—envy, hatred, persecution, and all the responses you want to avoid.

But My purpose for your life is to provoke hunger. Many will see and hunger for My reality.

Lord, I think you put Your finger on why I avoid liking myself. I want to avoid unpleasant realities like hatred and persecution.

Your human nature will always want to avoid them. I did not want to drink the cup of suffering in Gethsemane, but I chose to do so, just as you eventually will choose.

Why Don't You Like Yourself? 17

You may not choose quickly and never without a struggle, but ultimately you will choose as I did, because My life is at work within you.

*You see, my nature **has** overcome your old one. That, too, is a fact—not a fulfillment to be hoped for someday, but a reality now. Your lack of experience of this reality does not diminish its validity.*

Your realm of understanding is undergoing transformation. Trials have produced fruits you have long hoped for, and now the enemy wants to rob you of the joy and pleasure of those fruits.

*Inside, you are almost bursting with joy at the work I have done. You **like** the person you are becoming, but are afraid to give way and enjoy yourself.*

Go ahead! Enjoy yourself, just as you enjoy Me and together we enjoy our Father. Praise is the key which releases joy. Release all fear, and join Me in praise.

18 Like a Butterfly

Father, we praise You! We praise You for Your marvelous work in us. We thank You for making us the way we are. May Your kingdom come soon.

2

Why Do You Hurry So?

Why do you hurry so?

I don't know, Lord. It seems there is always so much to do and so little time. I can't even enjoy what I do because I worry about all the unfinished work.

Would you like to be free from that worry?

Think before you answer. Freedom comes by breaking a preconceived mold you have fastened around yourself. Are you willing to be changed?

Oh, Lord, I'm ashamed that I have to be given time to consider such an offer! I should respond gladly to anything You want to do for me.

20 Like a Butterfly

This is the mold that must be broken.

What do you mean, Lord?

Don't you see? You analyze yourself, trying constantly to fulfill an ideal image. Holding this ideal in your mind, you try to keep yourself prepared to meet all situations correctly.

What a hard way to live, Lord!

*It **is** hard. I want you free to be yourself, to respond to life with child-like spontaneity.*

Then something must be wrong with my idea of the mature Christian.

Your idea of the mature Christian is not My idea of maturity at all. That, too, is part of your mold.

Well, at least I have learned not to ask, "What do I **do**?"

I'm glad to see your smile. You are given the ability to laugh at yourself to relieve

Why Do You Hurry So? 21

tension and pressure. Do you remember the instruction to rejoice always? Rejoicing includes laughter, even at yourself. Learn to laugh with Me, and you will find joy in your mistakes.

Recall your children learning to walk. Did they make "mistakes" when they fell?

> No, Lord, and the scenes I remember are happy times, full of love. It was fun to see their delight in learning to walk. They could sense my pleasure, too, and they were eager to try again even after falling.

This is the pleasure you give Me when you fall and get up again. To make My joy complete, rejoice with Me when you fall, just as a baby laughs and clumsily picks himself up. Learn that we, too, can share a mutual joy in each other.

> This is good, Lord, but...

What has it to do with My original question?

Yes. Aren't we sidetracked from why I'm always hurrying?

Only momentarily. You needed a bit of encouragement before we could proceed.

Uh, oh. Are you about to hit me with something hard?

* * *

Lord, why don't You answer. I've offended You, haven't I? I'm sorry.

It grieves Me for you to doubt My love, but I hold no grudges, remember?

Let me explain why you stay so busy. Your hectic pace is caused by fear—fear and the need to experience My love.

What fear, Lord?

The fear of failure.

Why Do You Hurry So?

Fear of failure?

Yes, and the urge always to make a correct response is one of its symptoms. You stay busy, working to achieve perfection because you are afraid to fail.

Well, what's the solution, Lord?

Failure.

Failure!

Yes, failure, followed by a heavy dose of My love. Remember the baby learning to walk? If he were afraid of falling, he would never take the first step. Because of your love and encouragement, he has no fear and has learned to laugh when he falls.

So...

Slow down. Let others see your weaknesses, and don't be afraid to fail now and then. Be yourself, and you will experience the reality of My presence day by day.

Untruth in any form, whether pretense or hiding your mistakes, keeps you and others from knowing I live inside you.

Be free and open like a little child. Avoid deception, and don't look for darkness to hide under when you fall.

Don't you know, dear one? You are made of a strong and resilient substance that can withstand disapproval and persecution. But if you reject yourself, then you disagree with Me and lose your joy and strength.

Oh, Lord, thank You for teaching me. I love You so much!

3

Let's Talk about Burdens

Something wonderful is happening, Lord! I anticipate our times together and watch for opportunities to be with You.

I wish I had known sooner this wonderful relationship was possible. Serving You is easier, too. Before, I felt obligated and burdened.

Let's talk about that.

What, Lord?

Burdens.

I didn't expect that. I'm soaring higher

than a kite, and You want to talk about burdens. The word makes me uneasy.

It shouldn't.

You are going to teach me something new, aren't You?

You are going to learn a new truth about an old truth.

Is that parable talk?

Call it "think-it-over talk."

Okay, what new truth am I going to learn about an old truth?

What do you know about burdens?

I'm not sure how to answer. My mind is searching for biblical knowledge, but are You asking for personal experience?

Which would benefit the most?

Let's Talk about Burdens

That's hard to answer. I guess I'll give an answer I feel will be correct even though it's something I read somewhere. "Biblical knowledge should supersede personal experience."

That sounds good, but do you really believe it?

I know I should believe it.

But do you?

Lord, You're putting me on the spot. I feel like Peter when You asked him if he loved You. I'll just have to leave it up to You. You know my heart.

What if I said your heart is pure.

I would have trouble believing You.

Why?

Well, the Bible says evil things come out of the heart, and I've seen bad stuff come out of me.

Like a Butterfly

That's the old truth for which I am going to give a new truth. The old truth burdens My people and causes anguish and conflicts.

They know what they should be, and yet they see a difference between what they should be and what they think they are.

> Hey, You said, "What they **think** they are," not "What they **are!**"

I am glad you noticed.

> Lord, a Scripture is coming to mind! In Ezekiel 36:26, You promised to give Your people a new heart! Are You saying You've really done that? Do I really have a new heart?

A new creation should include a new heart, shouldn't it?

> Lord, tell me again! Do I really have a new heart? Is it really a good heart that good things come from?

> That's so wonderful I can hardly

Let's Talk about Burdens

believe it. Why didn't I know that before?

Yet with my mind, I did. I knew it was in the Bible, but now with You telling me personally, I really know. I really do!

Lord, I'm so happy I don't know if I can settle down for more teaching, but a question is forming in my mind.

If I have a new heart, why do I still sin? That is the biggest question in every Christian's mind. **Why do we sin?**

The spirit of your mind is not fully enlightened. Enlightenment does not come by intellectual knowledge.

Enlightenment comes by receiving Me. The more you receive Me, the more you understand. I am Truth. When you allow Me in any area of your life, I bring freedom and knowledge.

Then, do sinful acts show areas we haven't surrendered to You?

Yes, but it is the spirit of your mind that must be renewed. Your evil heart died with Me. You have a new heart now.

Lord, this is too much! I'm sorry, but I have to stop for a while...

* * *

Lord, I've been trying, and I think I understand. You're saying biblical knowledge is not enough without Your enlightenment and...

Lord, help! I can't get it!

Only if you think you need Me.

I'm sorry. I thought I could figure it out.

Just listen.

Let's Talk about Burdens

I have given you a new truth. You have just discovered your rebirth included a new heart.

The truth that the heart is evil is an old truth to you now, but still it remains in Scripture to do its convicting work.

For those who do not know Me, the heart is a storehouse of evil.

When anyone hears and receives Me, I bring new life, including a new heart.

Both old and new truths must be experienced for their power to be effective. Just because a truth has not been experienced does not mean the truth is ineffective.

> Lord, I'm having trouble! I'm having dirty thoughts! How can I have a new heart with dirty thoughts running through my mind?

Those are "fiery darts" from the wicked one. He would like to hide the truth of your new heart because he knows my people are like sleeping giants. He doesn't want you to wake up.

Thanks, Lord. Your words strengthen me.

I enabled you to use your shield of faith.

Hey, I did, didn't I? It works!

Your defense is made sure by My presence within you.

Lord, so much has happened in this conversation. Will You sum it up?

The burden I want lifted from you is the burden of trying to control an evil heart that does not exist anymore.

I can't describe what Your words do to me, Lord. An awesome thing is happening inside. I think I need to be quiet again for a little while.

* * *

Let's Talk about Burdens 33

Lord, I have been thinking, and I have another question. You said I need to be enlightened in the *"spirit of my mind"* (Ephesians 4:23). I know the term is biblical, but what **is** the spirit of my mind?

What are you using now, your spirit or your mind?

I don't know. I couldn't think this up by myself. My spirit must be active, but I'm using every brain cell in my mind, too.

Are your spirit and mind cooperating, but neither is dominating the other?

I think so, but this isn't easy! There is a terrific pull from both directions. My mind keeps trying to overrule and tell me I'm crazy. Then my spirit pulls the other way. It's hard to maintain a balance.

But you are doing it, aren't you? You are using the spirit of your mind. Your mind is receiving spiritual enlightenment, adding it to intellectual knowledge. This is the transformation, or renewing, of your mind.

This is it?

This is it.

My mind is being renewed just by sitting here talking with You. How can it be so simple?

It's that simple.

It can't be.

Oh, but it is.

I'm sorry, Lord, please excuse me. I have to stop again.

* * *

Why don't you say what you are thinking?

Let's Talk about Burdens 35

I'm scared to put it on paper.

Go ahead.

I feel uneasy. Something about this conversation bothers me. What You have just said seems to take away from the importance I place on the Bible.

Why?

I place heavy emphasis on Your written word. The Christians I respect most do, too.

We—well—Lord, the realization of what I am about to say shocks me!

Say it.

It's almost as if we worship the Bible! Is that wrong?

Have you ever tried to read a road map in the dark?

What do you mean?

You might as well try to read a map in the dark as to read My word with only your intellect.

I have given you the Bible to use as a map, as a light, and as food for your journey. Use it in that sense, but never forget your relationship is with Me, a Person, not a book.

> That scares me! If You are not speaking—and it takes all the faith I have to believe it is You—then I am having blasphemous thoughts.

It is to that extent your priorities are out of order.

Isn't the real problem one you have had before? Aren't you afraid of criticism?

> I guess I am.

Expect criticism. These words are for those who are starved for Me, not those who want their religious intellects fed. My people are hungry for Me, but they are laboring under

Let's Talk about Burdens

religious burdens I never imposed upon them.

Encourage them to listen to Me and let My written word provide confirmation to what they hear. Let them read and ask Me to be their teacher. Tell Me, what do you suppose I will feed them when they "dine" with Me?

*If they hear Me knock at their heart's door and open to Me, I will come in. I will fellowship with them and feed them, and speak My written words into their hearts. I will teach them just as I am teaching you. If they seek **Me**, there will be no conflict between Scripture and what they hear in the spirits of their minds.*

Lord, be patient with me, but I have to be sure I'm getting this straight. Throughout this conversation, Scriptures have come to mind, confirming what I hear.

You are not saying, then, that I don't need the Bible?

Not at all.

I say that studying and reading the Bible can become a heavy burden without the relationship we enjoy right now.

> You have lifted another burden, Lord. The burden of prayer. That's what I'm doing now, isn't it?

You didn't recognize this as prayer because our conversation is usually one way, while I do all the listening.

> Lord, if this is prayer, it's wonderful and not a chore.

"My yoke is easy, and my burden is light" (Matthew 11:30 NKJV), remember?

> Your yoke is so easy I can't tell I'm wearing one, and Your burden is so light I can't feel it.

> These have been the happiest days of my life.

4

Let's Talk about Words

Let's talk about words. I see your concern.

I think I talk too much, Lord. I have a compulsion to talk sometimes, and I try too hard to make people understand, especially about You.

This is not good.

You've never said that before. I'm scared.

Don't be afraid of truth. Truth is your friend.

I'll try, but I have butterflies in my stomach.

40 *Like a Butterfly*

What do you fear most?

> That I will make a mess of things and won't fulfill Your purpose for my life. I'm afraid You will set me aside.

Is that truly your greatest fear?

> Isn't it?

Your greatest fear lies behind that one. Would you like to see?

> I think so, but I'm becoming more frightened.

Nothing will be revealed unless you choose.

> Is this something I've hidden from myself for a long time?

Yes. Do you want it revealed?

> I'm still afraid, Lord, but let me see.

Your greatest fear is that I will disappoint you.

Let's Talk about Words   41

What a thing to say! I don't want to accept that. My first impulse is to deny it.

But You must be right. You don't make mistakes.

Yet, you doubt what I say is true.

Yes, in fact, I am beginning to doubt the whole conversation.

Don't run away. Let Me explain.

Okay, but I guess there is no use in trying to hide my feelings. I started this conversation with such expectation, but I feel let down now.

I **am** disappointed in You, Lord!

Disappointment has been inside all along.

I'm shocked, Lord, and yet I'm relieved to have the sin exposed. Every time the attitude surfaces, I push it back down. I'm tired of doing that.

42 Like a Butterfly

Rest while I tell you a story.

Once there was a little girl who loved her father with all her heart. She listened to him and believed his words. She was too little to know he was a man with faults and weaknesses like all men. He was her father, and she loved him very much.

Then gradually the realization came that his words were not always true. Often he did not keep his promises. She began to view him through eyes curtained with doubt and disappointment.

So deep was the little girl's disappointment that it caused her to be suspicious of the words of others. Words became empty boxes, little packages neatly tied up with nothing inside. Her own words often became empty boxes because they did not carry her true feelings.

Her fear and mistrust of words carry over to this day.

Oh, Lord, it's true! That little girl is

Let's Talk about Words 43

me! I always have been afraid of words. I get so frustrated when my words don't convey what I want to say.

Since I met You, I feel an even greater responsibility to speak wisely, and that adds more fear.

And yet...

And yet?

I have seen others helped by my words. What a joy! And people have helped me with their words.

The words You have spoken to me—look what they have done! Your words in the Bible are wonderful. But...

Deep down, there is still fear that what I have promised will not happen. You fear My words are empty, too.

How could I think that of You? I should know You will never fail me after all You have done.

44 *Like a Butterfly*

*You **should** know, and you try to believe, but a wounded spirit hinders you.*

> I didn't know the hurt was there, Lord.

Wounds of the spirit go deep and can be revealed only by Me.

> How do I get rid of the disappointment, Lord? I want it removed. I want to be healed.

Come with Me to a far away hill called Calvary. Can you hear My words from the cross?

> ***"My God, My God!***
> ***Why have You forsaken Me?"***
>
> (Mark 15:34)

Those words are not empty boxes. They contain all the disappointment suffered by mankind.

Watch as I put your disappointment in them. All your disappointments, you see,

Let's Talk about Words

became Mine. I carried them to death with Me.

You will never have to fear empty words again.

> You did a beautiful thing in me just then, Lord, thank you!

> The fear of empty words made me talk too much, didn't it? I can see that now.

Do you remember what the Bible says about well-spoken words?

> I'll have to find the verses, Lord. The book of Proverbs is full of beautiful descriptions!

"A man has joy in an apt answer, how delightful is a timely word."
(Proverbs 15:23)

"Like apples of gold in settings of silver is a word spoken in right circumstances."
(Proverbs 25:11)

"He kisses the lips who gives a right answer." (Proverbs 24:26)

46 Like a Butterfly

"A soothing tongue is a tree of life."
(Proverbs 15:4)

I notice a change in attitude.

Those Scriptures penetrate my heart! Something is different.

Disappointment restrained your faith. Now you are more free to believe.

Surely You had good reason for allowing the disappointment in my life?

I show My strength through human weakness. I will use your fear of empty words to produce meaningful words.

What a blessing!

I give abundant life, remember?

But let Me reveal your weaknesses. Most weaknesses hide under a masquerade of strength. You tried to appear skillful with words, didn't you?

Let's Talk about Words

I guess I did, but I didn't know how to make my words meaningful.

Trust Me to fill your empty boxes.

I am also taking away a tool for criticism. Understanding will take its place. Now, when you hear others speak empty words, you will know their needs are the same as yours—to receive living words from Me.

Thank you, Lord, for taking away the fear that You might disappoint me.

I remember a beautiful Scripture that expresses how I feel now:

"Now to Him who is able to do exceeding abundantly beyond all that we ask or think, according to the power that works within us." (Ephesians 3:20)

5

Almost Normal

Our first conversation was less than two weeks ago, Lord. What an amazing two weeks!

Not amazing, just almost normal.

These conversations are normal?

They're astounding! I want the whole world to know it's possible to talk with You.

They will.

Are You speaking of the time when everything will be revealed at the end of the world?

Here we go again! We are getting into

50 *Like a Butterfly*

one of those scary conversations where I don't have the slightest idea what You will say next. I have to hang on tightly to my sanity then. Why are some conversations easier than others?

You use your knowledge more than you use Mine.

There goes my faith! If that's true, I'm going to quit. I don't want to write anything if it doesn't come from You.

Perhaps we should review our past lessons. Didn't I teach you that you are part of Me?

Yes, You did, Lord.

Didn't I say that I use your hopes and dreams to fulfill Mine?

I remember.

Then what does it matter whether some of these conversations are drawn from your resources or from Mine?

Almost Normal 51

It matters a lot to **me**!

One thing I know: if I rely on myself instead of You, I get into trouble. I have been afraid I would get off on the wrong track and let my imagination run wild. I think it has finally happened!

Lord, if You really are talking to me, please let me know!

Rest with Me until your courage returns.

* * *

Assurance just came, Lord. I couldn't think up all this by myself. You are talking to me!

Where were we?

We were discussing our mutual resources. They will be used to spread the good news to everyone.

Like a Butterfly

You make things clearer than I do, Lord.

But I cannot accomplish My purposes without you. That idea crosses your mind sometimes. Why are you afraid of it?

Because I like it so much. Being needed makes me feel important, and that scares me.

You are important and needed. Our Father has chosen us. Accept His choice.

Oh, Lord, don't say "us" as if we are on the same level. I can't stand it.

My purpose is to change the idea you have of yourself. You must be free from self-consciousness.

When you are too aware of yourself, you do not allow Me to work through you as I like. Questioning whether your resources are from Me or from you hinders our work.

Lord, throughout this conversation, an

Almost Normal 53

idea keeps trying to surface, but I push it back down. I can't admit it.

Let it out. If the thought is wrong, it will be judged by My light.

Well, it seems You don't see anything bad or wrong with me at all. You make me feel that we are mixed together somehow. It seems, in Your eyes, there is no difference between us. I know You said we are part of each other, but I am such a poor image of You that I am ashamed to let myself believe it.

You have chosen to keep your eyes on yourself, not Me.

What if you did not have to make a conscious effort to do My will? What if you were free to live naturally?

That sounds great, but I'm afraid I would be in big trouble if I did. Isn't that the world's "do-your-own-thing" philosophy?

54 *Like a Butterfly*

What if your thing has become My thing?

Here we go again! You must see differently than I do.

Today, for instance, in several situations—one I'm particularly ashamed of—I lost my temper and yelled at my daughter. I didn't do a very good job of representing You then.

I have not given you the job of representing Me. I am asking you to allow Me to represent you.

Represent me? How?

Just as I did before. I came to earth to represent both God and man.

If you make a conscious effort to show God to others, you lose a natural quality and become self-conscious. Your walk is not natural. You walk like an acrobat carefully balanced on a tightrope.

Sometimes, I do feel like I'm on a

Almost Normal 55

tightrope—one slip and down I fall.

There is a better way.

Lord, if there is, I want to know it.

Be yourself.

I had a hunch you were going to say that, and I didn't want to hear it. Talking with You helps so much, but I'm still afraid to let go and be myself.

How do I do that? Just do whatever I want?

Do what I want, but be yourself.

Won't there be a conflict?

There will be no conflict. This is the way to discover the reality of your new self.

*The conflict you experience now is in trying to be one-hundred percent God. You must be one-hundred percent God **and** one-hundred percent human.*

56 *Like a Butterfly*

I didn't know I was trying to be God! That's terrible! I thought I was trying to be a good Christian.

And wait a minute, how can I be one-hundred percent God and human at the same time? That makes two-hundred percent!

Only if you see them separately.

Now I'm right back where I started! Do You mean that I, here in this ordinary body on earth, actually am a part of God—the all-powerful, supernatural God—who lives in heaven?

The way it was with Me is the way it is with you.

But, Lord, you're different! You're God's Son! You're God Himself. You're Deity. You're the One by whom and through whom all things were made!

I am also the firstborn of many brethren. Do you understand what that means?

Almost Normal 57

No, I must not.

In a family, is one brother related to the father more than another?

No, Lord, but...

In a family, does one child have less of the father's life than another?

No, Lord, but surely you aren't saying the whole set-up You had with the Father is the same one we have? Is it the same with us as it was with You?

The same.

Well, there sure is a big difference in our lives! Why is there such a contrast?

I knew who I was. You are just beginning to discover your true identity. The discovery will continue until you become fully aware. Your awakening is from the outpouring of my Spirit on earth as I give everyone opportunity to receive Me.

58 *Like a Butterfly*

Lord, this conversation is the deepest yet. I feel like a little child listening at the conference table of the wisest men on earth. Please go over all this again. An unbearable thought is forming in my mind.

I consider God and man as separate beings, distinct from each other. Is that right?

We were separate. You were in My image, but apart from Me. Now, all distinctions, all barriers are removed from those who receive Me. God and man are made one.

* * *

The penetration of this truth brought me to my knees. Many times I had read the good news, but now the nucleus of the message exploded inside me.

My mind still struggles to believe, but something has happened to my heart. Excitement stirs when I think of the "ages to come" for God's people. His grace is truly amazing!

6

The Baby Wakes

Lord, for two days, I have been reading our last conversation. My mind still struggles to believe You have removed all the separations between God and man.

This morning, I read that You are *"the firstborn among many brethren"* (Romans 8:29), and new understanding flooded my heart. You are my older Brother! You are still Lord, but we really are Your little brothers and sisters.

And our communication has been little more than baby-talk.

If this is baby-talk, I can't imagine what lies ahead.

You cannot, it is true. Eye has not seen and ear has not heard about the preparations made for you.

> Something is happening to me, Lord. I feel like I am slowly awakening.

My Spirit is stirring within you.

> I also see that if I try to judge whether I am using my strength or Yours, then I am not walking in faith.
>
> If I try to walk in the Spirit, my efforts become the focus of my attention, not the Spirit.

Well put.

> There is still so much I don't understand.

I am glad you are waking. Can you imagine the joy in heaven? All its inhabitants see My people beginning to stir.

They are like a delighted circle of family

and friends gathered around a long-awaited newborn child. They watch as the baby sleeps and makes only an occasional movement. Then the baby wakes and eager faces gather around, waiting for the first happy moments of recognition.

> Lord, that's exciting!

Greater joy is ahead. The child's growth is not measured by your terms. Knowledge of Me is the measurement used, and that knowledge can spread faster than blood courses through the human body.

Knowledge of Me comes through revelation given by our Father and is not limited by time or distance.

The sleeping child can become fully grown quickly.

> When You talk like that, Lord, I want to shout for joy! The time for us to go home is almost here, isn't it?

62 *Like a Butterfly*

It is.

I want to run in ten directions at once and try to get ready for Your coming!

Be still. Listen and watch for Me. I will come quickly as a thief in the night. To one who is alert and listening, a whispered call sounds like a shout in the ear.

Just as My call shall bring you to Me, so shall you be prepared by My Spirit-empowered words. Listen, and let Me bring the transformation you cannot produce by human effort.

Remember, I am the Word of God. I, Myself, communicate and transmit all that you need from the Father.

7

You Heard the Wrong Voice

Hey, Lord, I don't have to be alone to listen to You. Here I am riding with my husband through the mountains of Colorado. The car radio is playing and still we can talk, can't we?

I prefer our quiet times.

So do I, but I want to talk to You now, Lord.

It is not always necessary to talk.

Should I be quiet more, even with You?

Yes, and there is a reason.

64 Like a Butterfly

What is it?

I am teaching you good heavenly manners.

I'm so glad! My background didn't prepare me for the social graces. I'm insecure in earthly etiquette.

If you are comfortable with heavenly manners, you will never be uneasy in earthly etiquette.

That explains how a carpenter's son could be comfortable eating in a rich man's home.

Do you remember my visit to Simon's house? Why don't read that story now?

* * *

Lord, I'm embarrassed. I can't find the story in my Bible.

Why don't you ask Me where it is?

You Heard the Wrong Voice 65

I'm afraid to listen for something specific, Lord. If I hear incorrectly when we just talk like this, it's not so obvious.

Not obvious?

I'm getting nervous, Lord. What are You doing?

I am helping you increase your faith. Listen for the Scripture reference.

I'll try, but I really don't want to.

I can't hear you, Lord! There is just a jumble of words in my mind!

Be still. Listen.

I think I heard something, but I'm afraid to write it down. Let me look in the Bible first to see if it's right.

No, write it down first.

Well, okay.

66 *Like a Butterfly*

It's Mark 9:21.

Now, look it up.

Oh, Lord, it's wrong! That's not the right Scripture!

Didn't I hear You correctly?

You wrote what you heard.

But You don't make mistakes. What's wrong?

You heard the wrong voice.

That's terrible! I feel like ripping the page out! I acted in faith, believing You were speaking and look what happened. I can't hear Your voice after all!

* * *

I close the journal and do not open it for three days. Gradually, the Lord begins to comfort without

You Heard the Wrong Voice

speaking. I cling fiercely to my "map," the Bible, and understanding comes without words. I learn He is much more interested in developing a relationship than dictating to a recording secretary.

There will be times when I will misunderstand and not hear correctly, as in any relationship. Listening to the Lord will be an adventure that is not without risks, but removing my cocky confidence has eliminated one danger.

Finally, hunger to be with Him overcomes my reluctance to listen again.

* * *

Well, Lord, here I am, ashamed and not nearly so sure of myself. I hope You don't have to put me through something like that again.

It was necessary.

I am trying to see good in it, but...

Chastening was not pleasant?

68 *Like a Butterfly*

No, Sir, it was not.

And now?

All I want is to be close to You again.

Even if I do not speak?

Even if You don't. I don't want to go back to the way it was before, but anything is better than not being with You at all.

You withdrew from me.

I know, and I'm sorry.

Would you like to begin again?

Not where we left off, please. Can we just close this subject and go on to something else?

Wouldn't you like the confusion removed?

Well, of course, I would like the mess cleaned up. Excuse me, Lord, but that's

You Heard the Wrong Voice 69

how my mind records it.

What is your fear?

That I will make a mistake in listening to You again.

* * *

With that thought, fear rolls in again and overcomes. Another day passes.

* * *

Lord, help me!

Do you want to be helped, or do you just want relief from your discomfort?

I just want to get on the right track with You again.

Think for a moment. Can you see what I

have tried to teach you?

I guess not. All I can see is that I'm messed up. I'm afraid I'm not really hearing Your voice after all.

My worst fear is that You will ask me to hear something specific. If I fail again, Lord, I'll want to run away from You again.

This is your lesson.

What, Lord.

Learn to trust Me always, in failure and in success. I do not gauge success as you do. You look for results. I look for benefits.

Benefits?

Benefits for you and for others. Often the result that is so displeasing to you is a lasting benefit I work carefully to develop.

Maybe I'm standing too close, but I can't see any benefits from this little

You Heard the Wrong Voice

episode. I felt so foolish when I looked up the wrong Scripture reference.

Try not to exaggerate a small thing. Keep your perspective.

Lord, your answers are so frustrating! The answer to the situation seems simple to me. If only You will do something to reassure me that I am hearing Your voice.

Give me a sign or something to keep me from doubting again!

* * *

The age-old battle rages: my will against His, my demanding questions against His quiet resolve.

He wins, of course, using His ultimate weapon. Love sweeps over me and in an instant, He becomes my focal-point—not myself or my failures, but just Himself.

* * *

Lord, I'm hooked! I love You so much, I don't care what You do with me.

Your love is such a powerful force, nothing else matters. I want You and not what You can give me.

And I want you and not what you can give me.

You want me?

Yes, I want you. I do not care for your achievements. You, yourself, are important to me.

Then everything is okay between us?

Everything is okay.

Even though I sulked and pouted and acted like a child?

It is forgotten. Why don't you get out of that little hole of self-pity you dug for yourself and climb up here beside Me. I want to show you a beautiful view, but you can't see

You Heard the Wrong Voice 73

it from down there.

Lord, I don't know what you are doing, but I feel lifted! Here I am sitting close beside You!

Tell me what you see.

People! Hundreds of people. They move, running back and forth like ants.

Something is wrong with some of them, Lord. They are hollow and empty inside, like empty light sockets. I think they are supposed to shine, but there is no light in them. Somehow, the light void makes their emptiness seem worse.

Now I see an occasional person who is filled with light sprinkled throughout the masses of empty people. The ones with light are Your people, aren't they, Lord?

Can you see why you are the salt of the earth and the light of the world?

I see why, Lord. But you promised to show me a beautiful scene. Where is the beauty? Those empty people are not pretty.

Do you focus on the blackness or the beauty of the stars in a darkened sky?

Why, the stars, Lord.

Your beauty is My solace and comfort. You shine like a bright star in the midst of darkness.

Me? With all my failures?

I see each failure as an opening for light. Let your light shine through failure and success, but let it shine. Unhappiness comes from refusing to let out your light.

I want to ask You how to let out my light, but I know Your answer. "Be yourself." Right?

Be yourself. Admit your mistakes. Admit your successes, but be yourself.

You Heard the Wrong Voice 75

"Be yourself" is the theme of this whole thing, isn't it? Is that what matters most?

Our relationship is most important. Stay in My love. If you remain in My love, you will have no trouble being yourself.

8

Why Do You Harbor Hatred?

What do you ask of Me?

I don't know what to ask, Lord. I'm content just to be with You. I feel so satisfied. Is that wrong?

No, but I must ask you a question.

Why do you harbor hatred for Me in your heart?

Lord! Your words hurt so much I can hardly write them! Why did You do that?

I am not angry, and I intend no harm. I am using words like a surgical instrument.

78 *Like a Butterfly*

Well, You cut me deeply, Lord.

What are You doing?

You have an infection caused by an old wound of hatred. Hatred is foreign to your new nature and must be removed.

There is hatred in my heart?

I don't want you to be a carrier of this infectious poison.

Then get it out of me, Lord, please.

Be still. This is a delicate procedure, and you must cooperate while I probe gently with My words.

Will it hurt?

Not as much as you were hurt by the wound itself. Don't be afraid. Trust Me.

I feel better. The faith you gave me just then has a calming effect.

Why Do You Harbor Hatred? 79

Then I must ask another question. Why do you have no mercy toward those who hate you?

I don't understand. Who hates me?

Seldom do you see someone's hatred. The influence of hatred in your own life has blinded you to hidden hatred in others.

There are people who hate me?

If they hated Me, they will hate you.

Lord, I'm not aware of being hated. Have You protected me?

I allowed your blindness to act as insulation, but now it must be removed. You must be free to give mercy to those who hate you.

Lord, I'm more concerned about concealing hatred in my heart toward You. Do I really?

I thought You said I have a new heart.

80 *Like a Butterfly*

This sure looks like a contradiction.

Your heart is pure, and it motivates you to do good, but there is sin residue formed around wounds in your memory. This hinders your good motives. These wounds must be exposed and healed.

Now I see how sin affects, or perhaps I should say infects, a Christian.

I am glad you understand. When you see My purpose is not to punish or hurt, you are free to cooperate with Me and work out your salvation.

Is that what it means to "*work out your salvation*" (Philippians 2:12)?

Working out your salvation means never to stop receiving Me.

Let's have a demonstration.

My heart skipped a beat when You said that, but I guess I'm ready.

Why Do You Harbor Hatred? 81

Let Me expose the old wound first. I will not force My will upon you. If you choose, you may keep the wound covered. Nothing is hidden from Me, but you can resist My cleansing light.

> Help me to open myself, Lord. I'm still not sure what You intend to do.

I am going to show you a play in a theater. Do you see the stage?

> I do, Lord!

There are three characters are on stage: a small child, a mother and father. Do you see them?

> Yes, the child is holding the mother's hand.

Tell me about the father.

> He is taking the child's other hand. Oh, Lord! The parents are pulling in opposite directions. How terrible! The child will be torn apart!

82 Like a Butterfly

Lord, something evil is hiding in the darkness offstage. It enjoys what is happening. It hates all three!

This is the enemy, Satan. From the beginning his purpose has been to destroy you.

Keep watching. See what happens.

The child is in anguish, but the mother and father glare at each other and don't notice. Each is so intent on winning they don't see what they are doing to the child.

What does the child do?

A choice must be made to stop the terrible pull. What a terrifying decision for a little child! If only another way could be found!

But there is nothing to do but choose between the two.

Why Do You Harbor Hatred? 83

What happens?

> The child lets go of one hand. The choice is made. The conflict stops, but, oh, what a terrible price the child has paid.
>
> The child is hurt, deeply hurt, and cries inside, but still they don't see. They continue to glare at each other from a distance.
>
> Lord, is this little child me?

It is.

> Is this when the hatred began to form?

You tell Me.

> Yes! I had to have something to cover that awful torn-apart feeling. There was no other comfort. The enemy offered hatred as a covering, and I took it.
>
> Now I understand why Scripture says,

84 *Like a Butterfly*

> *"No one can serve two masters, for...he will hold to one and despise the other"* (Matthew 6:24). That's what happened to me!

Lord, I think I even hated both for forcing me to choose!

I am glad you admit the truth. Full confession will bring full healing.

Then, where were **You** when all this happened? Why didn't You make them stop fighting?

Oh, Lord, forgive me! I blamed You, too, didn't I? I let hate spread to my feelings for You. Please forgive me!

With that confession, I can turn up the house lights. Now, what do you see?

I see the mother and the father and the child, still on stage, but they are laughing and hugging and kissing each other.

Why Do You Harbor Hatred? 85

And, Lord, I see You, sitting on the front row, applauding and cheering.

What a happy scene!

Do you see why I hate sin? See how it harms you?

Sin is a destructive power that can hide only under the cover of darkness.

Lord, sin blinded me so much I couldn't see the love and affection that did exist in my family. I wish there had been more light. I wish I could have seen more clearly then.

This is why I ask you to let your light shine. The world needs your light and you deprive others when you withhold the light of truth.

Lord, You are so good! Your goodness is so beautiful, so refreshing.

Here comes a Scripture to my mind: *"Surely goodness and mercy shall*

86 *Like a Butterfly*

follow me all the days of my life" (Psalm 23:6). You have been chasing me, trying to catch me and give me Your goodness and mercy all my life, haven't You, Lord?

And mercy reminds me of Your second question. Now that I'm not blinded by hate, will I have mercy for those who hate me?

Yes, you have mercy. Choose to impart it.

Why do I have to keep choosing, Lord. Why don't You just do it for me?

Choose. Until the last breath, until the last step, choose.

Choice is your freedom, not a burden.

Believe I have chosen you and that I am responsible for the choices you make, and choice will not be a burden.

Discover you are free to impart mercy to all.

9

Wait on Me

The following conversation took place at a church retreat. After the morning chapel service, we were given forty-five minutes to be alone with the Lord.

I welcomed the opportunity because I was frustrated over contradictions in teachings, and I was impatient to get all the answers at once.

* * *

Lord, I need to talk to You right now. I need some answers quickly.

Wait on Me.

Wait for what?

Wait on Me. Be still.

> Those are negative words, Lord. "Wait" and "be still" mean "no" to me.

Did I say, "no?"

> No, but...

Your ways are being transformed to Mine, and you are learning to wait.

> Well, at least I have learned that the process of transformation is not in a set of rules and regulations.
>
> Teach me your ways, Lord.

My ways are simple. Apply the teaching you are given. Take the first step, and do what you know to be right. The next step will follow.

> Lord, You're so good! I keep expecting You to make me do something hard, but You keep on making everything simple and easy.

I feel like I'm waking from a bad dream. I have to force myself to shake off the bad feelings from the dream and wake up to the reality of Your goodness.

Hey, Lord, that sounds like something You would say. I'm getting so I can't tell my thoughts from Yours. They're all mixed up together.

That's us—all mixed up together.

Tell me about waiting, Lord.

What does waiting mean to you?

Dullness, boredom. I hate it.

I gave you a definition of patience. Do you remember?

You defined patience as "the state of relaxed learning."

Waiting can be a beautiful experience, also.

Like a Butterfly

What is your definition of waiting, Lord?

Waiting is anticipation. Anticipating goodness, anticipating freedom, anticipating wholeness. Waiting is anticipating Me.

I see something when You say, "anticipating," Lord.

What do you see?

I see an excited child looking forward to a holiday. I see eagerness and joyous expectation.

That doesn't sound so dull.

I remember that, as a child, waiting sometimes brought more happiness than the thing I waited for.

This will not happen when you wait on Me, but past disappointments keep you from the enjoyment of waiting now.

Disappointments in others, or in You?

*There is no difference in your inner self. Even the smallest child has a place where he files charges of offense. **All** charges are filed against Me in the deepest part of yourself.*

> I think I knew that deep down, but it hurts to hear You say it. I can see just a small part of the hurt You must suffer from having all those charges filed against Your loving heart.

Waiting is My comfort. I wait, anticipating the time when you will receive My love.

Now, would you like another definition? Would you like a definition of "time"?

> Yes, Lord, tell me.

I think I will let you enjoy the anticipation.

> You mean I have to wait for the definition?

Practice what you learned.

92 *Like a Butterfly*

A child enjoys ahead of time, doesn't he?

Try it.

I feel a little foolish, but here goes.

I expect Your definition of time will be fresh and new, something I've never heard before.

Go on.

I am expecting it to be simple and yet profound. I know I will enjoy telling others about it. Is that wrong, Lord?

It's not wrong to enjoy what I give you. Hang on to that, and don't let the enemy rob you.

What else do you anticipate?

I expect...

Oh, Lord, there goes the bell signaling the end of our quiet period! Our time

Wait on Me 93

together is over! It was so short. Where did it go?

I have given you a living illustration of "time."

Time is the limited opportunity given you to know Me. The purpose of your short span on earth is the same as the forty-five minutes given you this morning: to meet and know Me.

10

The Window of Faith

Lord Jesus, help me keep my mind on You. My thoughts are running this way and that.

* * *

Lord, my thoughts get worse the harder I try to listen. Won't You help?

* * *

Have I offended You? Why won't You answer?

* * *

Something is wrong, Lord. What is it?

I think you know.

96 Like a Butterfly

Okay, I'll admit it. Even with this display of emotion, I'm not really seeking You with my whole heart. I make a lot of noise about it, but part of me is still somewhere else, busy in other activities. Why do I do that?

The Christian life is frustrating, Lord! We have such high ideals, but when we try to reach them, they evaporate.

Forgive me, Lord, but I need to be honest. After our conversations, I'm often so emotionally high that I think I'll never come down again. But then, before I know what happens, I pull away from You, and down I go.

Things are better, I must admit. I can't give up or turn back, and I find myself plugging on no matter what happens.

Hey, Lord, are You laughing? What's so funny?

You are like a small child with a piece of tape stuck to his fingers—annoyed, but fascinated by his dilemma.

I'm afraid I don't see the connection or the humor.

Get your eyes off your sticky tape and look up. What do you see?

My mind is blank. What am I supposed to see?

Look around.

Literally?

Literally. Look around, what do you see?

Well, I feel foolish doing this, but I see the room I'm sitting in, the furniture, and the window with its view of the outside...

You want to teach me something about the window, don't you?

Tell me, which appears larger? The room or the view outside?

98 *Like a Butterfly*

The room.

Which is actually larger?

The outside is larger, of course, Lord. What are You saying?

I want you to change perspectives. Remember the days you were elated? What made the difference?

Well, if I apply what You said, my focus was outside myself—on You and on others.

Good! But there is more.

The happiest days are when I share what You have taught me, but how can I do that all the time? I have other responsibilities.

Am I an unreasonable person?

No, I guess the fault lies with me.

* * *

Lord, what have I done now?

* * *

Lord, I feel sick inside! I don't really believe my unhappiness is my fault. I think it's Yours!

I didn't know that ugly attitude was in me. That's it!

I am so tired of this up and down Christian life! If it has to be this way, then I need to know so I can accept it, but I am so tired of seeing promises dangled in front of my eyes when I can't reach them.

Forgive me for saying this! I'm appalled that all this stuff is coming out, but it feels good to be honest. You must have known my true feelings anyway.

Help me, Lord, help me!

100 *Like a Butterfly*

I wanted to help many times, but you did not listen.

Your problems are not new, and they are not unique. I experienced them also.

> You couldn't! You led a victorious life.

What is a victorious life?

> One that never yields to sin.

But is it a life subject to temptation?

> It must be, for the Bible says You were tempted *"in all points"* (Hebrews 4:15 NKJV). What does that mean?

It means that I experienced the same ups and downs as you do.

> You didn't!

I did, but I never departed from My Father's will—not in the up times or in the down ones.

The Window of Faith

Wait a minute, Lord, I can't get over this. You mean You didn't go around feeling victorious all the time?

Oh, even as I write those words, I remember You experienced sorrow and heartache, but I thought somehow You were different.

I thought life never touched You the way it does us. I thought life was easier for You since You are the Son of God.

Perhaps I should ask, what is defeat?

Well, it...

Give me your first thought, for that is your true response.

I wanted to say, "when I feel defeated," but I have been taught not to let feelings rule and was ashamed to say it. Lord, what is defeat to You?

Death.

Lord, You were victorious and triumphant over death. You weren't defeated.

Triumph came through the power of the resurrection, but My death was absolute and ultimate. I experienced the ultimate defeat for you.

You withstood defeat through all those temptations and then experienced defeat in the end—that seems unfair.

Death was not the end. Death was the beginning, and I want you to view your defeats in the same way.

Remember, "Except a grain of wheat falls into the earth and dies, it remains by itself alone; but if it dies, it bears much fruit" (John 12:24). The grain appears to be defeated by the heavy cover of dirt. However, its defeat is not the end, but the beginning.

As you sit in this room, its walls limit your vision. You have only a small view of the outside space through the window. This

The Window of Faith

represents your life on earth.

Because I experienced death, the ultimate defeat, on your behalf, you do not have to fear such defeat. You will never experience the blackness of hell, for I have given you a window of faith that cannot be covered. As you have noticed, "something" inside keeps your faith alive.

When you find yourself in what you consider defeat, enlarge your perspective. Look past the walls of your situation. Look through the window of faith, though circumstances may appear much larger than your small window.

Look and see that I have tasted the ultimate defeat for you. Never fear defeat, for any defeat you experience is not an end, but a beginning.

And, yes, the blame you gave Me for your defeated experiences is well-placed, for I have allowed them. Submit to My will instead of the anger the enemy offers, and you will enjoy peace.

Lord, I hope I can remember all this and learn to apply it...

Look again through the window. What do you see?

The beauty of green trees and blue sky, the peacefulness of nature.

Let that be your reminder. When you look through the window, remember the window of faith and the peace it brings.

11

The Meaning of Grace

Lord, will you please explain what grace means? I know the definition is "undeserved favor," but those are just words for my head. I need a definition that touches my heart.

Perhaps I can illustrate with a picture.

What do you see?

I do see a picture, Lord! I see a deep, deep canyon!

Look closely, because the canyon represents the gulf stretching between God and man.

Walk with Me to the edge. What do you see?

Blackness, awful, terrible blackness. It

looks like it contains nothing but despair and hopelessness. And it's so wide, Lord! I can't see the other side.

Tell Me what you see now.

I see You going down into that awful blackness.

Lord, I can't see You! Aren't You going to come out again, Lord?

There You are! You're coming out on the other side. You did it! You crossed over!

I want to shout, "Hooray for our side!" But, Lord, I'm still over here. How can I be where You are?

Look at your feet.

When did You put these shoes on my feet?

They're different from any shoes I've seen before, bright and shiny. They feel

The Meaning of Grace 107

good! I think I like them!

What are you wearing on your head?

A covering of some kind, close-fitting, but still flexible. What is it?

Don't you know?

It's my helmet of salvation, isn't it?

Would you like to inspect the rest of your armor?

I should be wearing a breastplate of righteousness, Lord, but I can't see it. That's the piece I need most. I feel vulnerable in righteousness.

You can't see or feel your covering of righteousness. You must believe Me when I say it is there and its protection is sufficient.

It sure would be good to see my own breastplate of righteousness.

You would spend all your time keeping it shined and polished if you could see it. This way is best.

> Okay, Lord, if You say so. Besides, I can see the belt of truth now. It's beautiful! Look! It makes light. I can see where I'm going with this thing. There is light all around me...

Why do you hesitate?

> I know what's next—the shield of faith and the sword of the Spirit. I almost dread to pick them up.

Why?

> They will be heavy and difficult to use. If I hold one in each hand, how can I carry anything else?
>
> The other pieces of armor are wonderful, but the shield of faith and the sword of the Spirit sound like big, heavy burdens.

The Meaning of Grace

This attitude can be changed now that it has surfaced, but there is another to be changed, too. Turn around, what do you see behind you?

> A wall! Where did that come from? It's high, Lord, so high I can't see over the top, and it goes wherever I go. I don't know if I like that thing behind me or not. I'm afraid it will close me in.

You expect the worst, which is another attitude I am changing in you.

The wall behind you is protection from the past. I place it there to protect you from the condemnation of past sins. Everything is for your good. My provisions bring freedom, not confinement. There is liberty in My Spirit, not restriction.

Now, here is your sword and shield of faith.

> I'm ashamed, Lord. I'm ashamed of my attitudes and ashamed I can't even see my shield of faith. I think my faith to listen to You just ran out, too.

110 *Like a Butterfly*

Use your sword, and strike the enemy of doubt.

Not me! I'm too little, and the sword is too big. You do it for me.

Try. You will be surprised how well the sword fits your hand.

Okay, I feel silly doing this, but here goes.

The Word of God says, *"Greater is He that is in [me] than he that is in the world"* (1 John 4:4). In the name of the Lord Jesus, I say to you, mountain of doubt, move away from me!

Lord, it's gone! The sword works!

And now I can see the shield of faith. Oh, it's big, Lord, as tall as I am. Lord, where is the handle? I can't find a place to take hold of the shield.

There is no handle. Simply step forward and take it by faith.

The Meaning of Grace

Okay, I don't see how I can do that without a handle, but you were right about the sword working, so, by faith I receive the shield of faith.

Now move your arm.

Lord, the shield is fastened to my arm! I don't have to hold on to it, it's fastened to me, and it's not heavy at all! It's a beautiful thing, covered with beautiful colors and jewels!

I am glad you like it. Each shield of faith is custom-made for its owner. Incidentally, your shoes will give you stability when you tell others the good news about Me.

I want the whole world to know about You, Lord!

Are you ready then?

Ready for what?

To cross the canyon.

112 *Like a Butterfly*

Lord, do I have to cross? I'm having second thoughts about that. Isn't it enough that You crossed over for me?

You don't really expect me to go down in that awful canyon, do You?

Walk to the edge again and look down. What do you see?

I see little lights down in the darkness, thousands and thousands of lights moving in a steady stream across the canyon. Lord, are those Your people?

They provide the only light and hope for those who want to cross and can't find the way.

Then I won't be alone?

You are never alone, but notice each light is surrounded by darkness. Each light has its own little place to illumine.

I've been all mixed up about grace, Lord. I thought when I first saw that

The Meaning of Grace 113

canyon, perhaps Your cross would make a bridge, reaching from one side to the other.

*My cross did reach from one side to the other, but only as I carried it. You see, I **lived** the span that separated God and man. My death on the cross absolved the penalty for man's failure to live that span himself. Your penalty has been removed and you have power to walk across the separation, but still you must cross over by faith to our Father yourself.*

But what about death? Do I just get transported over somehow when I die?

You are escorted safely through in death, but still you must cross. All provisions have been made for your safe crossing.

There is much you must learn about grace, but you are not ready now.

That's true, Lord, I'm not.

Why can't I sit still and listen all day

114 *Like a Butterfly*

to You? I can only stay for just so long and then I want to get away from You. Why am I like this?

Your cocoon of flesh prevents and holds you from Me. Find comfort in knowing you are struggling free, as the caterpillar struggles free from his old cocoon. You are experiencing your new life more and more. You are equipped and prepared for crossing the canyon. Now, cross and let your light shine as you encourage others to cross, also.

Glorify our Father in heaven.

12

Learning Me

Lord, Your heart seems heavy. Why are You so sad?

I watch my people running everywhere, always searching and striving for fulfillment.

Lord, we are caught up in endless pursuits that produce so little results, but we don't know how to stop. It's true, we are not satisfied people, but is that wrong? Shouldn't we always hunger for more of You?

The problem is indigestion, not hunger.

Indigestion!

You search and you strive to learn, stuffing

116 *Like a Butterfly*

yourself with religious activity. You study and feed from one expert after another, but never are satisfied. This is not true hunger for Me.

I'm afraid to ask what kind of hunger we have. I dread your answer.

Your response reveals a curiosity to receive knowledge without paying the price.

You see, there is a price to be paid in learning Me. Learning Me is very costly.

*You may learn **about** Me through much effort and expended energy. You may even receive knowledge another has gleaned by paying the price. While his knowledge will be genuine and lasting, yours will produce only temporary benefits. You cannot learn Me without personally paying the price.*

What is the price, Lord? Our lives?

What is your life? Many offer their lives and yet give very little.

Learning Me 117

I feel foolish, Lord. My first reply was, "all my will, all my personal desires," but the words seem empty.

What does my life represent?

The complete giving of yourself, your thoughts, motives, emotions and energies. Giving your life is spending all that makes up you.

I sense there is real energy in such giving, Lord. I remember the story of the woman who touched the hem of Your garment. The Bible says You felt power go out from You. You were spending Your life then, weren't You?

But, Lord, what has this to do with learning You? Do we learn by spending our lives?

And why do You keep saying "learning You," instead of "learning about You"? Is "learning You" becoming acquainted with You as a person and learning Your ways?

There are many who want to learn My ways of life. They grieve Me most because they become fascinated with the benefits of their learning and ignore Me.

They assume they are attaining earth's ultimate knowledge of Me and dismiss their lack of fulfillment, thinking they must wait until they reach heaven for more.

> Well, Lord, what **is** learning You?

Living My life, thinking My thoughts, experiencing My suffering.

> I don't know how to do that, Lord. I remember Scripture says I must lose my life to find it, but I must admit that the words are rather meaningless.
>
> How do I exchange intellectual knowledge for real experience?

Pay the price.

> Tell me again, Lord. How do I pay the price?

Abandon all reservations and spend yourself. When you look at someone, see them with all your heart, mind, and soul. When you listen, hear them with all your heart, mind, and soul. When you talk to someone, speak with all your heart, mind, and soul.

Do you mean total concentration?

Not merely mental concentration, but a giving of all the energy of your life to others.

That doesn't seem possible! How can I give myself so completely? That would bring about complete exhaustion. There would be nothing left of me.

It is true, there would be nothing left of you. But as you give yourself so completely, you will experience My life as never before.

Looking, you will see as I see. Listening, you will hear as I hear.

With no shield of self-protection, you will experience reality. You will learn Me.

Lord, I still picture such intense giving as leading to some kind of breakdown. Such a life doesn't seem practical.

It is not possible without the rest I give. Remember the times I went away to be alone with My Father? I found such refreshing joy in His presence there was no danger of exhaustion or death prematurely.

Oh, that word "prematurely" seems to say exhaustion and death **will** be the eventual result.

*Not exhaustion as you know it, and not death as you think of it. However, a complete spending of life **is** the result for one embarked on the pilgrimage of learning Me.*

Now are you able to see why there are so few willing to pay the price?

13

Speak the Truth

Lord Jesus, help! I'm overwhelmed by an impossible schedule that would take two people to meet. I feel crushed under a mountain of responsibilities, and I don't have energy even to begin. I really need Your help.

Yet, I'm almost afraid of Your answer. I hope You don't just tell me to be patient, for this is one time I need a miracle desparately.

Let Me rephrase your request: "Lord, leave me alone, but change everyone and everything around me."

Ouch! That stung a little, but I do see Your point. Okay, change me, Lord—but please do it quickly!

122 *Like a Butterfly*

Here is your miracle: speak the truth.

What truth, Lord?

Any truth. Speak what you know to be truth. You are under a deceptive cloud of discouragement which will lift at the first light of truth.

Okay, I'll try.

First, I know that I belong to You, and You are mine. I know that I have been redeemed by Your shed blood, and I am Your child.

Second—and Lord, You must be giving me these words—I know my situation is not new. 1 Corinthians 10:13 says so: *"No temptation has overtaken you but such as is common to man; and God is faithful, who will not allow you to be tempted beyond what you are able, but with the temptation will provide the way of escape also, that you may be able to endure it."*

Speak the Truth 123

You have overcome the world, and I just remembered the victory that overcomes the world is faith—my faith in You! (See John 16:33 and 1 John 5:4.)

Oh, thanks, Lord, I'm getting my eyes back on You. You are the object of my faith, and if it rests in You, then I can't fail! The situation is not hopeless! Praise God, that's good to know.

Somehow, it must be possible to live with demands on my time and strength and yet come out a winner. How do I do it, Lord? You've restored my faith, and I believe victory is possible, but now how do I win?

Release all your ideas of strength and efficiency, and accept the fact there always will be excessive demands.

You think that somehow you can become smart and efficient enough to meet all the demands on your time and strength. Let that thought go.

124 *Like a Butterfly*

Excessive demands always try to consume like the roaring lions they are, for Satan uses ordinary circumstances to rush you into his snares.

Your idea of efficiency is not Mine. You see efficiency as the ability to meet all the needs and responsibilities that arise smoothly and capably.

My weary one, the stress of trying to be efficient drains your strength more than anything.

What if you were free from the ambition to be efficient? What would happen?

> I'm afraid I would laze around and get nothing done. I hate the pressure, but I keep telling myself I work better under pressure.

Only a slave works better under the whip!

> I do feel driven sometimes, Lord. When I can't stand any more, I just want to run away.

Speak the Truth

Don't run. Turn around and face each demand for your time and strength. Stop and look at each one. Make them walk in an orderly procession before you, one at a time, for your inspection.

What do you see?

> It sounds crazy, but I see a house that demands to be kept in perfect order. How dare it! I own it. It doesn't own me!

> I see work that demands to be done, appointments that must be kept, telephones that have to be answered, and needs that demand my immediate attention.

> Lord, I never realized circumstances were ordering me around. Now I know why I felt driven. What do I do?

Let Me handle them.

> Gladly, but how?

When a demand in any form approaches, send it to Me immediately. Don't be compelled or forced. I never force you into anything. I lead. I do not push.

If you find yourself being forced, stop and make a close inspection of the demand. Often, that will send it fleeing, but if not, pass it on to Me.

I may alter it and present it again in the form of work for Me, but I will not allow it to drive or threaten you.

Lord, will you review all this, please?

First, when clouds of doubt and discouragement come, dispel them with truth. Speak truth, not the enemy's lies of defeat.

Second, when you are overwhelmed by too many demands, do not ask for the demands to be taken away. Absence of battle is not victory. Instead, understand that excessive demands are part of the world in which you live. Always there will be more than you can do. When you accept this fact, you can

Speak the Truth 127

begin to deal with the demands.

Face each demand squarely. Look it over well. Choose either to accept or reject it.

If you choose to accept it, I will convert the demand to an opportunity to work for Me. Then you may work at it heartily with joy and thanksgiving.

If you choose to reject the responsibility or set it aside temporarily, then do so with the freedom of choice I have won for you. Trust Me to guide in decisions, and don't let indecision become another snarling lion.

As you face each demand with willingness to serve me, I will give you ability to discern its merit. Remember, I want you to make the choice and not let circumstances drive you.

Now, do you feel better?

> Oh, yes! Thank you, Lord! You are a wonderful teacher. I love You!

128 *Like a Butterfly*

Begin then. Begin to face the demands one by one. See that I have overcome the world for you.

14

Look Back with Me

Look back with me, see how far we have come.

> It seems I made very little progress, Lord.

You first wrote, "We made very little progress." Why did you cross it out?

> If little progress was made, it's my fault, not Yours. It's not right to include You in my failures.

Oh, but I am a big part of your failures.

> Lord, You never fail!

But I am with you in failure and success. I never leave you for one moment.

130 *Like a Butterfly*

I feel good when You say that, Lord. Tell me more.

Sometimes the most difficult task is to persuade you to believe simple facts. If you will believe I am with you always, and let Me plant this truth in your heart, your anxiety will disappear.

Then, help me to believe, Lord.

Listen to My story.

A man and woman journeyed to a distant country, traveling many days and miles. As they approached their destination, they grew weary and considered stopping short of their goal. They were very tired. After they sat and discussed their situation, they did a very foolish thing.

What, Lord?

They decided to go back.

Go back? Wouldn't that be harder?

Not to their reasoning. They decided the hardships had been too great and surely would become much harder the nearer they came to their destination. They decided they were too weak to proceed into greater difficulties.

Who told them the difficulties would be greater?

They reasoned so.

But they didn't know the future. Hey, Lord, I sense a moral in this story.

The moral is to beware of discouragement as you approach your goal. Don't dishonor Me by becoming bitter or discouraged when you meet trouble. You have come too far to turn back.

Oh, Lord, I wouldn't turn back.

Then, why are you casting a backward glance over your shoulder? Why second guess decisions you have made and actions you have taken? Why punish yourself

Like a Butterfly

needlessly for failures and mistakes?

How can you proceed if you keep looking back?

>Lord, I get so impatient! I am eager to see more change in myself and others.

So am I, but the answer is not found in looking back and complaining.

>If you don't want me to look back, why did You ask me to look and see how far we've come?

I want you to take one good look at the past, but don't look with fear and discouragement. Stand very close beside Me. Now, turn around. What do you see?

>I don't really see anything with my eyes, Lord, but I have an impression You are standing there. I can't see my past at all, just You!

Good. Now turn to your left. What do you see?

Look Back with Me

I see You again!

And to your right?

You're over there, too!

Can you guess what lies ahead?

You must be there, too, Lord. What are You saying?

Don't measure progress by accomplishments or experiences. Measure progress by Me.

I don't understand at all.

Good! If you could reason everything with your mind, then you would measure progress by learning.

Shouldn't I be concerned about my Christian growth?

My goal for you is very simple. Enjoy Me as I enjoy you, and together we enjoy our Father. You come nearer this goal each time you forget yourself and enjoy Me. Often you

134 Like a Butterfly

block our enjoyment by complaining about all your faults.

> I thought I was just praying about them. Besides, don't You want me to be honest and admit my faults?

Allow my Spirit to convict and correct. Then real change will take place. Is your complaining helpful?

> No, Lord, not really.

Let Me do the correcting then. That's My job. Can you trust Me with it?

> What if I don't hear or pay attention?

I know how to get your attention. I repeat, will you trust Me with the job of changing you?

> I gather You want a decision.

That's right. You need to get this settled. Will you trust Me completely to make all the necessary changes in your life?

Okay, Lord, the offer is too tempting to pass up. Yes, I accept! I trust You. In fact, how glorious! What a relief!

Now I am free to enjoy You even more. How wonderful! I love You, Lord!

And I enjoy and love you.

Now, my beloved, let's turn our attention to our Father and enjoy Him.

15

The Listening Ear

*The listening ear is not an instrument
That can be tuned or sharpened
To a fine point,
Nor is it a letter box
Whose flag can be run up and down
At a moment's whim.*

*It is like a fragile rosebud
Opened by unseen hands,
Slowly,
Petal by petal.*

*The listening ear is the result
Of time spent
Alone
and apart
With the Master.*

*It is born out of the rest and peace
Found while sitting at His feet,
Satisfied and content
Just to be near
And accepted by Him.*

*It knows no formulas for listening,
And cannot describe to another
The mechanics of hearing.
Neither can it explain
Why or how the Master speaks.*

*But to one who catches sight
Of the Champion of beauty
And is drawn near
By the cords of His love,
Listening becomes an excuse
And simply a reason
To remain for a little longer
In the presence of the Lord.*

*Listening becomes a contrived
Opportunity
To savor the taste
Of His goodness*

The Listening Ear

*And to enjoy
The aroma of a life
Broken and poured out in sacrifice
From an alabaster box
Of perfection.*

*The listening ear is found
Leaning in love and friendship
Against the bosom
Of its Lord.*

*It is discovered in the closeness
Of daily communion
With Him.*

*And, the listening ear is found
Lingering near the Master,
Awaiting His arising
And His call to come away
To be with Him
Forever.*